Fight
the Good
Fight

Fight
the Good
Fight

by
Gayland R Jones

BONNEVILLE BOOKS ™
Springville, Utah

Copyright © 2001 Gayland R. Jones

All Rights Reserved.

No part of this book may be reproduced in any form whatsoever, whether by graphic, visual, electronic, film, microfilm, tape recording, or any other means, without prior written permission of the author, except in the case of brief passages embodied in critical reviews and articles.

ISBN: 1-55517-561-9
v.1

Published by Bonneville Books
Imprint of Cedar Fort Inc.
925 N. Main Springville, Utah, 84663
www.cedarfort.com

Distributed by:

Typeset by Virginia Reeder
Cover design by Adam Ford
Cover design © 2001 by Lyle Mortimer

Printed in the United States of America
10 9 8 7 6 5 4 3 2 1

Printed on acid-free paper

> Library of Congress Cataloging-in-Publication Data
>
> Jones, Gayland R.
> Fight the good fight / by Gayland R. Jones.
> p. cm.
> ISBN 1-55517-561-9 (pbk. : alk. paper)
> 1. Church of Jesus Christ of Latter-day Saints--Missions. I. Title.
> BX8661 .J66 2001
> 266'.9332--dc21
>   2001003916

Table of Contents

Introduction	vii
Prepare Yourself to Serve	1
Spiritual Preparation for a Mission	1
Ten Ways to Cultivate Personal Spirituality	6
Quotes	7
Ten Points of a Successful Missionary	9
Self-Motivation	10
The Process of Prayer	11
Six Key Elements to Receiving Answers to Our Prayers	16
Ten Physical Reactions to Prayer	17
Quotes	17
Utilizing the Holy Ghost	19
Near to Your Heart - Poem	21
Quotes	22
Bearing Testimony	25
Quotes	27
Obedience	29
Faith	33
Quotes	38
Book of Mormon	41
Traits of a Good Teacher	42
Boldness	45
Work With All Your Might	46
The Plan of Power	47
The Harvest Time is Now. Open Your Mouth and Do Something Big!	50

Don't Quit	54
Quotes	54
Leadership Through Example	59
Five Keys	59
Christ	61
One Solitary Life	61
Never a Better Friend - Poem	64
Love	67
Quotes	69
Companions	71
Geese "V" Formation Helps Birds in Flight	71
Miracles	73
Return With Honor	77
The Marks of a Man	77

Introduction

"Fight the good fight of faith, lay hold on eternal life, whereunto thou art also called, and hast professed a good profession before many witnesses." (1 Timothy 6:12)

As a missionary, you are called of God. A living prophet of our Heavenly Father gives you this very special assignment at this time in your life. You become a special witness of our Lord and Savior Jesus Christ. As His witness, you testify of Him and teach His message. However, there is another being, or spirit, out there trying just as hard to thwart these plans and this message. His name is Satan. He dislikes the message of the gospel. Satan is trying to stop people everywhere from grasping on to the good and truthful things in life. He will do anything in his power to try to stop you.

When I was serving in a mission office, my companion and I left one afternoon to work. While knocking doors, we found a lady at home. Her husband was a truck driver but was not at home. We discussed the gospel with this lady and she felt the Spirit. I felt good about her reaction to the Book of Mormon, and she said that she would read and pray about it. We went back two days later to check on her progress and to talk with her. She came to the door but would not let us in. She said that she had read a little of the Book of Mormon and was feeling good. Then suddenly, as she was reading, her child fell out of its stroller and cracked its head open on the floor. She blamed the incident on the Book of Mormon. She said that things were fine until we showed up with that book. I know that it was Satan who put these thoughts into her head.

The missionary field is a constant battlefield. This battlefield covers the entire earth. Every day the forces of good and evil are at work. As a missionary, you will be able to actually see and live these battles. While in the service of our Heavenly Father, you must fight, for a fight it is! We must all be united to win this fight.

"The things of God are of deep import; and only time, and experience; and careful, and ponderous, and solemn thoughts can search them out.

Thy mind, O man! if thou will lead a soul into salvation, must stretch as high as the utmost heavens, and search unto and contemplate the darkest abyss, . . . thou must commune with God" (Joseph Smith, Jr., Teachings of the Prophet Joseph Smith, comp. Joseph Fielding Smith [Salt Lake City: Deseret Book, 1976] p. 137).

Prepare Yourself to Serve

Spiritual Preparation for a Mission

The "average missionary" requires four to six months to make the transition from self-centered John Smith to genuinely-interested-in-others, spiritual Elder Smith. Any missionary may save three to four months of this transitional adjustment, as he begins his mission, by following these suggestions:

1. Read the *Book of Mormon* at least three times.
2. Read the *New Testament, Doctrine & Covenants, Pearl of Great Price, A Marvelous Work and a Wonder, Jesus the Christ,* and *Articles of Faith.*
3. Memorize the first discussion completely.
4. Pray vocally for ten minutes both morning and night (three months).
5. Bear testimony weekly in some way to a non-member during the last three months before leaving.
6. Slow down, or stop dating during the last thirty days (avoid being alone).
7. Repent and confess all iniquity to your bishop.
8. Control your thoughts.
9. Turn off car radios and home stereos during the final two weeks.
10. Fast (for specifics) twice during the last sixty days.
11. Omit sex-oriented or foul language movies, rock

concerts, and dances.
12. Rise at 6:00 A.M. and retire by 10:30 P.M. for sixty days (D&C 88:124).
13. Study scriptures and discussions one to two hours for sixty days (6:00 to 8:00 A.M.).
14. Learn shopping, cooking, and ironing from Mom.
15. Develop a ten minute exercise program (exercise each weekday for thirty days), and get a haircut.
16. Read "The Joseph Smith Story" four times.
17. Write your personal testimony in six copies of the *Book of Mormon* and give them to non-member friends.
18. Receive your Patriarchal Blessing (fast for twenty-four hours prior).
19. Start your missionary journal thirty days prior to departure. Record your feelings about your preparation.

    I have a personal experience to share about preparing myself to serve my Heavenly Father on a mission. I hope that the story can benefit you in your own preparation.

    After high school, I decided to attend Southern Utah University. I had scored a "20" on the English part of the ACT test in high school, and that should have been enough to CLEP out of a college English class. However, they changed the requirement to a "21" just that year, so I had to take the class. I really should not have been there, but I pondered on the idea that Heavenly Father might have wanted me to be there. It could have been for a purpose.

    Our class was small and our teacher was excellent. She made sure that we interacted in small groups and got to know everyone. I met a girl named Jeanette Olsen a few weeks into the course. She was very beautiful, and I wanted to get to know her. My mom, for some reason, was pretty worried about my being at college. She thought that I might meet some people that did not have the high standards I did and that I would get mixed up with them. She was just being protective like most mothers are. I wrote a poem to Jeanette asking her to meet me after class. I was scared, but things turned out okay. Jeanette thanked me for the poem and said that it was very beautiful. She had never received anything like it. I found out that she only lived a block away from me, and we agreed to go on our first date.

I picked her up, and we drove to the bowling alley. We played a few games. She was quite good, but my ego would not let her beat me. I had to maintain my "manly" image. Next, we drove to Kentucky Fried Chicken for a good "home-cooked" meal. We then decided to go for a walk on campus and just talk. I really wanted to get to know her better, and I thought that this could be the time. She had asked me earlier if I had other poems that I had written. I told her that I did and agreed to bring them along so that she could read some. I also brought a little cassette player to play some songs (I wasn't a dummy). We walked around for a while, then we sat down on the lawn to relax and talk. We conversed about school, our families, where we were from, and things we liked. Suddenly, out of the blue, the theme of religion came up. I wasn't planning on that at first, but I did want to know what church she belonged to. She was very open about those kind of things, and she explained that she belonged to The Assembly of God. I was taken back a little and did not quite know what to say, yet, I knew in my heart that this could be a very good learning experience. I was taking the LDS Institute Missionary Preparation course at the time and felt like I could use what I was learning to help her.

We saw each other in class every day, and I looked forward to talking with her more and more. I definitely wanted to discuss religion, but because she was very attractive, I also wanted to discuss our relationship. We studied together, went on dates, and just "hung out" as friends. Finally, one day I just decided to make her a deal. I told her that I would go to her church if she came to mine. She thought that sounded fair. However, she didn't know what I had in store for her.

On Sunday we drove out of town a couple of miles to the Cedar City Assembly of God. As I walked in, the members treated me very friendly. We sat down and almost immediately the music started playing. Everyone, except me, jumped to their feet and they started singing at the top of their voices. I felt a little uncomfortable because I had never experienced anything quite like that before and had to chuckle inside. The pastor got up and gave a discourse, then, a few members went up to a little altar and started to pray—I think—I did not fully understand what they were doing. The meetings finished, and we went to the car and left.

A few days passed and I was still planning on taking Jeanette to our church; but, I wanted to take her on Fast Sunday, and it was not for another week. In the meantime, she started having a few problems with her church. The members had a few disagreements, and she told me that things just were not like they were in her church in Salt Lake. She decided to stop going for a while which was bad news for her but good news for me. I knew that Heavenly Father was preparing the way for something great.

Finally, the long-awaited day came for us to go to "my" church. I knew that she would be impacted by the meeting, but I did not know how much. As Sacrament Meeting started, we could feel a strong spirit. Then, one by one, the college-age members got up to bear their testimonies as if they knew they had to testify to someone in the congregation. I got up and shared my feelings also. After the meeting, Jeanette mentioned that she felt good inside. She could not believe that all of these kids were her age, and that they felt so strongly about religious topics. She knew some of the members and talked to them between meetings. I do not think she was ever quite the same after that day.

* * * *

As the days passed, Jeanette pondered the things that she heard and felt on Sunday. Her comments showed that she had meditated on certain gospel principles. It was amazing to me that she believed in so many of the same concepts of the gospel that I did. She had a few LDS roommates that knew about her church experience and tried to set a good example for her and answer any questions she had.

* * * *

One weekend she decided to go home to West Valley City, Utah. She must have really hashed things out with her parents while she was there, because when she returned to Cedar City, she immediately wanted to go for a walk with me. I did not know what she wanted to talk about, but I knew that it was important. We strolled into a few residential areas as she explained everything that she had talked with her parents about. I just stood in awe as she said that her mom had been through two divorces and had married a third time. She told me about many of her childhood experiences. Then, with a pause, she mentioned that she had been blessed, baptized, and confirmed in the Mormon church. She explained how she could only remember a little about Primary. I was astonished as she told me her story. Afterwards, I just blurted out, "You're a member, you're a member!" She actually was a member, but just very inactive. I was extremely happy!

* * *

From that day on, I could not help but think that the Lord knew what would happen. All of those times that Jeanette and I talked about the gospel, all of those times that we read the scriptures, and even all of those times that we prayed, He knew what was in store for Jeanette Olsen. I was just there as an instrument in His hands, and I thank Him very much for that wonderful opportunity.

The story was not over yet. She went on to accept callings in the Church and grew in leaps and bounds. She was learning every day and sharing her experience with others. After all was said and done, her mom and step-father were married in the temple. Jeanette Olsen herself was married in the temple for time and all eternity.

Ten Ways to Cultivate Personal Spirituality

1. Do I read the scriptures daily (2 Nephi 32:3)? Do I "nibble" or do I "feast"?
2. Do I really pray (converse with God) and not just say prayers (Alma 34:17-27; Matt. 6:7)?
3. Is my fasting meaningful; (D&C 59:13-23; Matt. 6:16-18) and is it coupled with prayer?
4. Do I go to bed early (seven hours of sleep) and get up early (D&C 88:124)? Do I practice "mind over mattress"?
5. Am I essentially a happy person (D&C 31:3; 68:6)?
6. Do I work hard (D&C 31:5) and "thrust in my sickle"? The Spirit isn't lazy.
7. Am I more concerned about *how* rather than *where* I serve (John 13:4-16)?

8. Do I love everyone, even my enemies, and keep romantic feelings in the proper perspective (John 13:34-35)?
9. Do I strive for unity with others, and between my ideal and actual self (John 17; D&C 38:27)?
10. Do I share my testimony with others (D&C 60:2, 62:3)?

Quotes

Every LDS male who is worthy and able should fill a mission (Spencer W. Kimball, CR, April 1974, p. 126).

Should every young man fill a mission? The answer has been given by the Lord. It is yes. Every young man should fill a mission. (Spencer W. Kimball, Regional Representative's Seminar, 4 April 1974.)

Proclaiming the gospel is one of the three missions of the church (Gayland R Jones, District Meeting, Tandil, Argentina, April 1992).

The past is behind—learn from it. The future is ahead—prepare for it. The present is here—live in it (Thomas S. Monson).

Two years to serve it and a lifetime to think about it (Anonymous).

In missionary work, as in all else, preparation precedes power (Gordon B. Hinckley, Regional Representatives Seminar, April 1987).

If you don't have a goal, you can spend your whole life

running up and down the field and never scoring (Anonymous).

A missionary needs the confidence of a tightrope walker, the commitment of a marathoner, the enthusiasm of a salesman, and the courage of a mountain climber (Ed J. Pinegar).

Be careful how you live, you may be the only Bible some people read (Anonymous).

Living a good life is like shaving—no matter how good you do it today, you still have to do it again tomorrow (Anonymous).

It is not necessarily the will to win, but the will to practice (LaVell Edwards).

As I sat down to ponder on a few missionary ideas one day, I realized that my brother Lync's missionary farewell was approaching soon. He had asked me if I would give a talk. I had responded that I would participate in the meeting with the family. I wanted to share some experiences and stories with my brother, and help him to get ready in any way that I could. We had discussed some topics before and enjoyed some good times together; however, I had not really shared with him some of the most important tools that he could use to be an effective missionary, so, I began writing a list of keys that all missionaries should acquire. Having served in the Argentina Bahia Blanca mission, I began thinking of some advice that I could give to my younger brother. I came up with a personal list of keys that I call "The 10 Points of a Successful Missionary."

Ten Points of a Successful Missionary

1. *Self-Motivation.* Your parents are not there with you all of the time to tell you what to do. You are on your own, and you have to make your own decisions. No one is making you do it. I believe that this is the most important tool that a missionary can have.

2. *Power of Prayer.* This is how we communicate with God (2 Nephi 32:8-9). This process is how we gain a testimony, acquire the Spirit, and make decisions.

3. *The Spirit.* (D&C 50: 13-14, 17-18). Talk from your spirit to their spirit! This is how your investigators gain their testimonies.

4. *Testimony.* Always bear your testimony! This is a very powerful way for the investigators to feel the Spirit and know the truth (D&C 58:47,59).

5. *Obedience.* It is the first law of heaven (D&C 130:20-21). The Lord is bound when we do what He says. The "White Bible" discusses very intricately the mission rules.

6. *Faith.* Alma 32:21. Ether 12:6. Faith is a strong belief that causes action.

7. *Learn the Discussions, Book of Mormon, and scriptures; then, teach them.* "I told the brethren that the Book of Mormon was the most correct of any book on earth, and the keystone of our religion, and a man would get nearer to God by abiding by its precepts, than by any other book" (Joseph Smith). President Benson's three reasons why the Book of Mormon should be a lifetime study are: it is the keystone of our religion, it was written for us, and it helps us draw nearer to God.

8. *Boldness.* Romans 1:16. Acts 4:20, 29, 31. Peter and John. Be bold and always open your mouth!

9. *Hard Work.* Psalms 62:12. Your work pace should

persist through the cold in the winter and the heat in the summer. Wake up early and go to bed promptly as directed by the mission rules.

10. *Be a Leader.* Lead by Example. Work the longest and hardest. See the most people. Teach the most discussions. Baptize the most converts.

You are a part of the great army of the Lord (D&C 64:33); fifty thousand missionaries strong.

Self-Motivation

People can be motivated by love or by fear; however, the motivation that I am talking about here is self-motivation. As a missionary, you are on your own with only the counsel of your companion and Heavenly Father. Your parents are not telling you what to do, and you are not required to do anything; but you need to remember that you are serving your Heavenly Father, and this time is His time.

I have a helpful hint on being self-motivated—set goals. Goal-setting is the strongest human force for self-motivation. If you want something bad enough, you will do whatever it takes to achieve that goal. Therefore, set goals and keep them, and you will be on your way to being self-motivated. You have to wake up on time, study, leave on time, work hard, and do all that you are called to do. You just have to do it! If you are not self-motivated, you will accomplish nothing. Thus, I believe that self-motivation is the most important tool that a successful missionary can have.

The Process of Prayer

"Oh, our beloved Father in Heaven, bring about the day when we may be able to bring in large numbers as Ammon and his brethren did, thousands of conversions, not dozens, not tens or fives or ones, thousands of conversions. The Lord promised it; He fulfills his promises.

Our Father, may we move forward with Jesus Christ as our advocate to establish the Church among the inhabitants of the earth. May Jacob flourish in the wilderness and blossom as the rose upon the mountains. May we merit the promise that the Lord will do things that we can hardly believe. May we improve the efficiency of our missionaries, each bringing thousands of converts into the Church. Please, Father, open the doors of the nations. I pray this in the name of Jesus Christ" (Spencer W. Kimball, Regional Representatives Seminar, April 3, 1975).

This was a great and tremendous prayer that President Kimball offered. One can really feel the Spirit and the power here! If we all pray, and continue to pray, as illustrated in this prayer, the Lord will bless us beyond all comprehension. The missionary work will move forward as the "stone cut out of the mountain without hands" and roll forth to encompass the entire earth, and "the God of heaven shall set up a kingdom, which shall never be destroyed: and the kingdom shall not be left to other people, but it shall break in pieces and consume all these kingdoms, and it shall stand forever" (Daniel 2:44-45).

In the Missionary Training Center, we had great training on how to be an outstanding missionary. Our teachers emphasized that we could not teach by the Spirit unless we had already received a testimony by the Spirit as it says in Doctrine and Covenants 50. Throughout my life I have always had a testimony of the truthfulness of the Church, Joseph Smith, the Book of Mormon, Christ, and the prophets. But, I wanted a reconfirmation of these things and a stronger testimony. So, I studied these things out in my mind and pondered them. But, the most important thing that I did, and that anyone can do, is to pray. In that moment at the side of my bed, the Spirit overcame me, and I felt the Spirit take control of my body. I felt a tingling sensation and cold chills. It gave me a burning feeling inside. I knew then that I could start my labors in the service of my Heavenly Father. This experience was how I gained an unshakable testimony through the power of prayer which would be the means of converting many people into the Church. My patriarchal blessing manifested to me that my testimony would be the powerful tool that I would use (D&C 8:2).

When you personally feel these things, you will become a special witness of the things I am telling you—things that I have experienced and the miracles I have seen—that they are true, because you will have these same burning feelings in your heart.

In the *Book of Ether* in the Book of Mormon, we read the wonderful account of the brother of Jared and his experiences of praying to the Lord. As you remember, the Jaredites had built eight barges in which to cross the ocean, but they had a problem. The barges would be closed up against the great waves of the sea. There would be no light, and how could they travel without light? The brother of Jared went to inquire of the

Lord about this situation. The Lord responded, "What will ye that I should do that ye may have light in your vessels?" (Ether 2:23). In other words, the Lord said, "Come on, brother of Jared, you have got to search out an answer and get back to me with your best idea for a solution." We must create a plan and put forth effort. How often do we try to avoid effort or struggle as we pray for spiritual help and direction?

Understanding that principle, the brother of Jared went to work and melted out of the rock sixteen small stones. He had to climb the mountain, make the stones, and polish them, following his plan. Then he went to the Lord and said, "Touch these stones, O Lord, with thy finger, and prepare them that they may shine forth in darkness" (Ether 3:4). Touching the rocks is all the Lord did. *That was the most important part, but the brother of Jared had to do ninety percent of the work.* We, too, must do everything that we can to bring to pass our righteous desires before we call on our Heavenly Father for assistance. He will do the part that we cannot do for ourselves.

The mechanics of prayer are quite important, but many people do not think about them or understand them. Prayers should be offered in secret, with humility, in a kneeling position, often with fasting, and unceasingly. You have probably eliminated bad prayer habits, such as excessive repetition or allowing your mind to wander during prayer. You should also recognize that you must have a sincere purpose and pray with real intent.

Some other imperative points about receiving answers to prayer are to: 1) prayerfully acquire all of the information possible, 2) study the issues out in your mind, 3) make a decision, and 4) offer this decision to God for His approval. These steps are what I call "The Process of Prayer." If we do not follow these steps, we may not receive answers to our prayers. The important actions are: *staying on our knees, asking, listening, waiting, feeling,* and *pondering. Being in a hurry, asking God to make the decision for us, and not waiting for an answer,* are three of the major reasons why more people do not receive answers to their prayers.

Two other fundamental aspects to remember are to keep your prayers simple and to keep your requests specific. I truly believe that many of us do not get answers because we ask too much and too fast.

Perhaps an experience that I had will illustrate the "Process of Prayer" and the power that comes from it. I was called into the office to be an assistant to the president (A.P.) about a year and a half into my mission. A month later, we had Elders Lynn A. Mickelson and John B. Dickson of the Seventy come to our mission for a couple of conferences. They taught us how to get the investigators' attention, how to teach the discussions more effectively, and how to be better missionaries. They told us that they expected more from our mission, and set up some reachable, but at the time, seemingly high goals.

After the conferences and plenty of discussion with my companion and President Finlinson, we all decided that we would continue to dedicate everything that we had to the Lord to further his work. Elder Fisk and I were the A.P.'s and we wanted to be examples to others in the mission. We set up some specific goals in line with the counsel of the Elders of the Seventy. We also tried to finish most of our work in the office early so that we could go tracting for longer periods of time during the next few days. As we went to bed that night, we laid out a simple, yet very specific, plan on how we would focus our efforts to accomplish these goals.

* * * *

After lunch the next day, and during the siesta, Elder Fisk

and I conversed a lot on all of our preparations for a successful mission. We wanted to please our Heavenly Father. Humility was very prevalent in our bottom-floor apartment that day. As we began to gather our scriptures and discussions for the afternoon's work, a solemn feeling swept over the quiet room. We knelt down by our beds and poured out our hearts to God. Elder Fisk prayed first, and asked that we would work hard, follow our plan, and utilize the Spirit. Then, I prayed that we could be examples to the other missionaries, and find some large families so that we could reach our goals of all those baptisms.

We left our apartment with humble hearts, but with a renewed sense of courage and trust. We drove to the other side of town and began knocking doors. We approached the first door, but after a few knocks, no one answered. We walked down the sidewalk to the second door and knocked on it. A young girl in her teens came out of the house and approached the gate. We explained who we were and asked to talk to all of the members of the family. The mother came out and invited us in. We were glad to see some hospitality. She had us sit down in the kitchen, and then she tried to get everyone to come in and hear what we had to say. Pretty soon, many doors were opening and closing from all angles and areas of the house. My companion and I just sat there in disbelief as we waited for all of the family members to arrive. Finally, the mother nodded that this was probably all of them for now. We began the conversation and found out that three families lived in the various rooms of this rather large house. There was a total of twelve people who heard the first discussion that day. The Lord truly blessed us! The last thing that I had asked for before we left our apartment that day, was that we could find a large family. After that exciting day, we were well on our way to baptizing many people that month and reaching our goals.

As we follow these principles and move up each rung of the ladder, our prayers will become more powerful and more meaningful. We will be strengthened, have the faith to move on, and actually receive answers to our prayers. Encompassed within "The Process of Prayer" are some key elements to receiving answers to our prayers and recognizing them as answers.

Six Key Elements to Receiving Answers to Our Prayers

1. Believe: Exercise faith, doubt not, and truly believe.
2. Repent: Sacrifice, pay the price.
3. Work: As if all depended on you.
4. Pray: As if all depended on God.
5. Prepare: For intense trials of your faith.
6. Expect: To see the arm of the Lord revealed in your behalf.

Now, as we implement these elements, they will ensure that we follow "The Process of Prayer" and that we begin to recognize the answers to our prayers. The recognition of the Spirit, when it is trying to tell us something, is a very valuable skill to have mastered. In fact, it might be the most notable and significant part of prayer. All of us have different personalities, likes, and dislikes. We are all different, and so the Lord and the Spirit will touch us in our own, individual way. We need to remember that we will not all react to the Spirit's stimuli in exactly the same way, or to the same degree. The ideas and feelings listed below are various ways that our Heavenly Father will speak to us and answer our prayers. The "Fruits of the Spirit" spoken of in Galatians 5:22-23 are other responses from the Lord.

Ten Physical Reactions as Answers to Prayer

1. A burning in one's bosom. It also might be a feeling of warmth all over one's body.
2. A quaking frame. This would be a slight trembling of the body, like a chill or a shiver, except that it isn't cold.
3. A still small voice.
4. Crying or weeping.
5. Enlightened mind or sudden ideas.
6. Peace in the mind and heart.
7. A constraining or impression not to say or do a specific thing.
8. A stupor of thought. This reaction is a sense of confusion or anxiety.
9. Comfort from distress or sorrow.
10. An awakening to the understanding of one's sins.
    (Blaine & Brenton Yorgason—"Receiving Answers to Prayer").

Quotes

When you find it the hardest to pray, pray the hardest (Gayland Jones).

Seven days without prayer makes one weak (Anonymous).

If the seat of your pants wears out before the knees, then you are going about things the wrong way (Anonymous).

Prayer is the lock of the night and the key of the day (Anonymous).

If you want to talk to God—pray. If you want God to talk to you—read the scriptures (Gayland Jones).

How can you expect a million dollar answer from a ten-cent prayer (Anonymous).

Utilizing the Holy Ghost

One of the greatest feelings in the world is when you are in the MTC and you sing "Called To Serve." The Spirit is so prevalent there, and you can feel the goosebumps on your arms and the hair raise up on the back of your neck. Being in the MTC with the desire to be diligent in recognizing the Holy Ghost, is a great start on utilizing this critical and influential tool.

While serving in the office, I had an overwhelming experience about feeling and using the Spirit. Elder Fisk and I left one summer afternoon to go and knock doors. During the middle of the summer, the weather is quite hot in Argentina. The worst part about the environment there is that it is so humid and sticky. That weather did not bother us, though, and we drove to a location where we had never been before. We decided to check out the neighborhood and meet some new people. These people would have a chance to know us and understand that we were in the area.

For the first hour or so, the missionary work was taking its normal course: some of the people did not want much to do with the gospel, so they sent us on our way; others were at least polite and paid attention for a while. Still others let us give a discussion and desired to learn a little about Mormons. We had some small successes by contacting a few people and acquiring some investigators for our finding and teaching pools. As we were walking along the sidewalk by a rather large cement wall, we both suddenly stopped in the shade of some trees. We felt that we should be somewhere else. We took out our small map of the area and decided to go to a street called Primera Junta. The street was a few blocks southeast of where we presently were.

As we began to walk there, we started talking about how we felt. It was kind of weird that we would change and go to a different location. Finally, we arrived at the spot, looked around and saw mostly white houses. We knocked on the first door. A girl came out and we told her who we were. She seemed nice and called her mom to come to the door. The young girl invited us in, and the mother immediately called her other daughters in to listen to us. We had not formally met the mother, nor discussed anything prior to our visit, yet she wanted everyone to come and listen.

We gave them the first discussion. They believed most everything that we taught them. The eagerness and anticipation was surely felt in that room. They acted as if they had found something that they wanted most deeply and had been searching for a long time. That discussion was the smoothest and most fulfilling discussion that I had on my mission up to that point. We left their house smiling! We had just found some "golden" investigators by stopping, listening to the Spirit, and following His whisperings.

This is a poem that I wrote as an expression of my feelings about the Holy Ghost. Sometimes we have those ponderous and thrilling moments when we are inspired. I feel that this poem gives some powerful insights on the Spirit's character.

Near to Your Heart

It's the start of a brand new day and you're up and you're ready to go.
You breathe the nice, fresh air outside as you watch the sky from below.
You see the sun's head over the mountains now and springtime is here.
You feel so happy inside because life is so clear.

And do you know why you feel this way? Because the Spirit is there to help you choose.
He opens your mind to the good things in life, and with him you'll never lose.
He's near to your heart and just touches you so right.
Quiet, but powerful whisperings that are hidden from your sight.

A friend of friends who is gentle, who's love and peace is the start.
These are the marks of his character that he presses so near to your heart.
Many people feel it but just don't quite know,
What this feeling is and how it controls your soul.

They're always searching for a clue but can't find out where it's at.
To crack the case of a mistaken one and get him back on track.
This is where the Spirit steps in, the faithful thinker but yet very sly.
Who is there for you always so that you can gain eternal life.

The warm Comforter testifies that the gospel of Christ is true.
He sends a wonderful sensation that tingles through and through.
So if there's a reward, run to win and achieve.
His Spirit talks directly to ours, now that's a prize to believe.

In my last area we baptized an older gentleman. He was a very special, humble person. The Sunday after his baptism he came to church acting like he was quite excited. When I asked him what made him so happy, he replied that he was paying his fast offering for the very first time. He also wanted to let me know that when I confirmed him a member of the Church and bestowed on him the Holy Ghost, he felt "fire." I responded, "You felt what?" He repeated, "I felt fire!" I thought that was a very interesting way of describing how the Holy Ghost makes you feel.

Quotes

There is one language that is understood by every missionary: the language of the Spirit. It is not learned from textbooks written by men of letters, nor is it acquired through reading and memorization. The language of the Spirit comes to him who seeks with all his heart to know God and to keep His divine commandments. Proficiency in this language permits one to breach barriers, overcome obstacles, and touch the human heart (Thomas S. Monson, Ensign, May 1985, p. 68).

Being able to have the Spirit of the Lord with you and being able to transmit it to your investigators is the single most important element in the conversion process (Gene R. Cook).

They may forget what you said, but they will never forget how you made them feel (Carl Buehner).

But the Comforter, which is the Holy Ghost, whom the Father will send in my name, he shall teach you all things, and bring all things to your remembrance, whatsoever I have said unto you (John 14:26).

But when the Comforter is come, whom I will send unto you from the Father, even the Spirit of truth, which proceedeth from the Father, he shall testify of me (John 15:26).

The Holy Ghost shall be thy constant companion, and thy scepter an unchanging scepter of righteousness and truth (D&C 121:46).

And by the power of the Holy Ghost ye may know the truth of all things (Moroni 10:5).

Angels speak by the power of the Holy Ghost; wherefore, they speak the words of Christ. Wherefore, I said unto you, feast upon the words of Christ; for behold, the words of Christ will tell you all things what ye should do (2 Nephi 32:3).

And the Spirit shall be given unto you by the prayer of faith; and if ye receive not the Spirit ye shall not teach (D&C 42:14).

Bearing Testimony

A testimony of the gospel is the sure knowledge, received by revelation from the Holy Ghost, of the divinity of the great latter-day work. This testimony comes when the Holy Ghost speaks to a person's spirit. It comes when the whisperings of the still, small voice are heard by one's inner self. When you receive a testimony, a feeling of calm, unwavering certainty follows.

When I bear my testimony, I include five truths: 1) that Jesus Christ is the Son of God and the Savior of the world, 2) that Joseph Smith was a Prophet of God and he restored the gospel, 3) that the Book of Mormon is the word of God and was translated by the prophet Joseph Smith, 4) that The Church of Jesus Christ of Latter-day Saints is the only true church on the face of the earth, and 5) that our prophet today, Gordon B. Hinckley, is a prophet of God.

The prophet Alma, in the Book of Mormon, bore his testimony: "And this is not all. Do ye not suppose that I know of these things myself? Behold, I testify unto you that I do know that these things whereof I have spoken are true. And how do ye suppose that I know of their surety? Behold, I say unto you they are made known unto me by the Holy Spirit of God. Behold, I have fasted and prayed many days that I might know these things of myself. And now I do know of myself that they are true; for the Lord God hath made them manifest unto me by his Holy Spirit; and this is the spirit of revelation which is in me" (Alma 5:45-46).

I believe that one of the greatest testimonies ever given was that by Elder Bruce R. McConkie in his last General Conference. I think that he knew he was going to die soon and he shared with the world what he knew to be true. His testimony is very impacting:

> "I am one of his witnesses, and in a coming day I shall feel the nail marks in his hands and in his feet and shall wet his feet with my tears. But I shall not know any better then than I know now that he is God's Almighty Son, that he is our Savior and Redeemer, and that salvation comes in and through his atoning blood and in no other way" (CR, April 6, 1985, p. 12).

Elder Lynn A. Mickelson of the Seventy came to our mission and held a conference. Just after his talk on Testifying with the Spirit, my companion, Elder Maughn, and I went into the downtown plaza of Bahia Blanca and stopped a man on a street corner. We taught him the first discussion in about twenty minutes. He knew that the words we spoke were true, because the Spirit was there and we testified strongly. He said that he felt like Christ was there with us. I really felt the power! I knew then that this method works, and testifying with feeling is the only way to convert.

As missionaries, we need to bear testimony to everybody. The scriptures say, "Let them preach by the way, and bear testimony of the truth in all places, and call upon the rich, the high and the low, and the poor to repent. And let no man return from this land except he bear record by the way, of that which he knows and most assuredly believes" (D&C 58:47, 59).

You need to talk from your spirit to their spirit. This feeling impacts the person and marks him for life. Testifying with the Spirit is the only way that the investigator will know the truth and want to be baptized. Therefore, strengthen your testimony through prayer and study and carry it with you wherever you go. Never be afraid to bear it to those with whom you come in contact.

Quotes

The greatest testimony you will ever bear is your life (Anonymous).

You might prove doctrine from the Bible till doomsday, and it would merely convince a people but would not convert them . . . Nothing short of a testimony by the power of the Holy Ghost would bring light and knowledge to them—bring them in their hearts to repentance. Nothing short of that would ever do (Brigham Young, JD, 5:377).

Remember that "it is a day of warning, and not a day of many words." If they receive not your testimony in one place, flee to another, remembering to cast no reflections, nor throw out any bitter sayings. If you do your duty, it will be just as well with you, as though all men embraced the gospel (Joseph Smith, HC, 1:468).

Did I not speak peace to your mind concerning the matter? What greater witness can you have than from God? And now, behold, you have received a witness; for if I have told you things which no man knoweth have you not received a witness? (D&C 6:23-24).

Obedience

We wear black name tags on which is written the name of Jesus Christ. We are His servants. We were called by Him (see 3 Nephi 5:13). We represent Christ and we have to act in a manner that pleases Him. It is essential that we have the appearance and the behavior that He would like us to have, so that we're not made hypocrites by wearing our name tags every day. This account brings us to obedience. It is the first law of Heaven. It makes us worthy and produces happiness. Obedience gives us power.

A while ago, I had the beautiful experience of working close to and with my mission president—President Reese Finlinson from Oak City, Utah, and I was able to capture the complete and total vision of the mission. During one month, the mission surpassed one hundred baptisms. Truly the Lord conceded to us much success. Nevertheless, the following month everybody got lazy and submitted to the temptations and tricks of Satan. They started to fall into error and disobedience. We saw cases of missionaries who got in accidents and broke their bones because of their negligence. Others fought with members, rode motorcycles, did not wake up or go to bed on time, quit working as much, and offended people when they chastised them for being negative. Can you imagine what happened in the mission? Yes, we had problems with obedience. The quantity of baptisms went down sharply until we only had about seventy a month. Some tried to justify this and make excuses for not having greater success and baptisms.

That was all right for them, I guess. But, what did a prophet of the Lord say concerning this? ". . . to obey is better than to sacrifice" (1 Samuel 15:22).

We have our ups and downs in the mission field. I will draw a diagram to illustrate a few points: We begin with two Obedience Lines on which we draw a wavy line. The wavy line represents our ups and downs over time. The shaded areas represent blessings. We can receive blessings by surpassing either one of the Obedience Lines.

```
to receive greater blessings -->-----------------------------
to receive blessings         -->-----------------------------
```

Next, we have the norms and rules of the mission, as given by our respective mission presidents. We are responsible for implementing them if we desire blessings and success. Many missionaries live the law of obedience just enough to reach the first Obedience Line.

```
                                 -----------------------------
Lower law (mission norms) -->-----------------------------
```

Finally, we arrive at my favorite point—the point of higher laws. If we really desire to receive tremendous blessings and success beyond our wildest imaginations, we need to live the higher law. It seems simple, and it is. However, it can also be quite hard at times.

```
live the higher laws -->-----------------------------
                        -----------------------------
```

We can motivate ourselves to live these higher laws. It depends on the results that we want and the attitude that we have. Consider the mission of Ammon, who was an example of obedience to higher laws. Ammon went to the land of Ishmael and served King Lamoni and the Lamanites. He saved the king's flocks and slew his enemies. After recovering and gathering up the king's sheep, he returned and commenced to ready the king's chariots and horses for travel. King Lamoni was astonished, for Ammon was faithful and obeyed all of the king's commandments to execute them. He obeyed with exactness and lived a higher law.

We can and should do the same. Let's be completely obedient! Let's do more than obey the norms and rules of the mission! For example, we do not have to always leave our apartments at 9:30 A.M. We can leave earlier and sacrifice a little. The prophet Joseph Smith said, "I made this my rule: when the Lord mandates something, do it." This motto can also be our norm. We need to demonstrate to the Lord that we deserve His blessings. He says, "If ye love me, keep my commandments" (John 14:15). Also, the Lord is bound when we do what He says (see D&C 82:10). So, that means that He is able to bless us when we obey Him.

Faith

Three things are necessary for a rational and intelligent being to exercise faith in God unto life and salvation. "First, the idea that He actually exists. Secondly, a correct idea of His character, perfections, and attributes. Thirdly, an actual knowledge that the course of life which he [or she] is pursuing is according to His will" (Lectures on Faith, 3: 3-5).

Faith is the first principle of the gospel. Faith should be centered in the Lord, Jesus Christ. It is a power, a gift, and a conviction that gives us confidence and makes us act. We have to be worthy to use this faith. The prophet Joseph Smith teaches us that faith is what motivates our daily activities. He said that faith is a principle of power and the motivating strength of our internal actions.

According to Hebrews 11:1,6, faith is the confidence in things hoped for that are not seen but are true. The apostle Paul is speaking here about faith and being pleasing to God. If we truly believe with conviction and then act on those feelings, God will reward us.

Will we leave our families and journey thousands of miles if we do not believe in a worthy cause? Will we try to study and learn if we do not believe that we will obtain knowledge and wisdom? Will we go out and do missionary work every day, in the heat or cold, if we do not expect to touch people's lives? If we study the scriptures carefully, we will learn that faith is a profound and sincere belief inside our souls that motivates us to do good. Each day we work on the things that we hope for, even though at that moment we cannot see the final results. These examples are all about faith.

The apostle Paul, in speaking about faith in Romans, chapter four, verses five and sixteen, explains that faith is a quality of righteousness. By doing our Heavenly Father's will and obeying all of His commandments, we will be able to acquire more faith. This eternal law is based on the concept of righteousness.

In Ether 12:6, Moroni is speaking about this same topic. This scripture says that you do not receive a testimony until after the trial of your faith. First, we receive commandments and covenant to keep them. Then, we experience hard times and trials. If we continue to do as we have covenanted, we will be blessed with much faith and a greater witness. Going on to verses thirteen through fifteen, and seventeen, it says, "Behold, it was the faith of Alma and Amulek that caused the prison to tumble to the earth. Behold, it was the faith of Nephi and Lehi that wrought the change upon the Lamanites, that they were baptized with fire and with the Holy Ghost. Behold, it was the faith of Ammon and his brethren which wrought so great a miracle among the Lamanites. And it was by faith that the three disciples obtained a promise that they should not taste of death; and they obtained not the promise until after their faith."

I read a book about faith a little while ago. It said that we should obey the commandments, live righteously, and set goals by writing them on paper. It is important to write our goals on paper so that we can check our progress periodically. Then, we should pray constantly about our specific goals and never doubt. However, we should not suppose that all we have to do is ask in prayer. Remember ". . . faith, if it hath not works, is dead, being alone" (James 2:17). Faith is actually made perfect by works.

Faith is not only to believe in something, but to act on what one believes. It is essential that we are doing all that we can so that the things that we hope for, and for which we pray, are fulfilled. It is necessary that we act on what we believe because we must do our part. We need to be "doers of the word, and not hearers only" (James 1:22).

In my second mission area, I was called to open up half of a city, an area that consisted of seventeen thousand people. Both my companion and I arrived on the same day. We did not know of any members in this city. We also did not know where the chapel was. We did not have any investigators—we were pretty much starting from scratch. The thought kept running through my head that I was called to that area by a man of God. My mission president put us there for a reason, and I just had to find out what that reason was. I kept thinking that there are certain people waiting for certain missionaries, and there were some souls in this city waiting specifically for me. I had much faith that something good would come from our being there.

We began to cover our area and get acquainted with the streets and the people. We met new people every day and let them know that the Mormons were in town. We also searched through the area book and familiarized ourselves a little with a few members and past investigators. We visited the church one day and knew that we would be spending a lot of time there, since I was first counselor in the branch presidency and my companion was second counselor. After about a week, things were running quite smoothly. We worked very hard and knocked on many, many doors. Many people in that city knew who we were, and others were soon going to find out.

One morning we went to some of the outlying houses to speak to the residents there. After knocking for a while, I thought to myself, "Wow, we sure are not having much luck here." I conversed with my companion about the situation, and decided to knock two more doors on the corner and then go somewhere else. The funny thing was that the second door was the one we were waiting for. We met the Carabajal family. We knew that this house was the reason why we were placed in that city, because after two months we were both transferred. The father of the house answered the door and talked to us for a couple of minutes. He decided that we were good young men and that maybe we could help his family. He invited us in, but wanted us to talk more to the others in his family. I think that he felt a little embarrassed because he had some drinking buddies over at the time. We sat down and began to teach everyone. I realized that about twenty people were in the room.

The second-eldest daughter came out from the back room, and the father yelled to us and said, "There she is, help her." He began to explain that she was married for a little while, had a child, and then her husband left her. From that time on, she acted like she was mentally and physically handicapped. She hardly ever spoke, and it seemed like she did not understand what anyone was saying. Also, she walked with a limp. We directed our conversation towards her at first, but then we noticed that she never really seemed to be paying attention to us. Four of the daughters and the mom all enjoyed the various topics that we discussed. They talked amongst themselves and were very enthusiastic. They all exhibited signs of interest in the Book of Mormon as we assigned them passages to read, and they absorbed everything. We even talked quite a bit about worldly things. They liked some of the music we liked, and they asked us questions about ourselves, hobbies, and what we did in the U.S. One of the girls did a lot of things with her friends, and the big thing for them to do was to ride the moped. We established a good friendship right from the start.

Later, as I was thumbing through my journal, which I

wrote in every day for two years, I read about the events that transpired from the day that we met this family. After showing two films and having the second discussion, we bore our testimonies and committed them to be baptized. On the thirteenth of February I wrote, "I hope, and actually I know, that we will baptize them." I believe that during the two months that I served in this city I exercised incredible faith.

We finished the rest of the discussions, and they continued to attend church. We enjoyed some good times together. They were getting excited and preparing for the big day. Finally, the day arrived for their baptisms. This day was a very pressing, yet eventful, day. We went down to the chapel to begin filling the baptismal font. It usually takes about three hours to fill up so we decided to go and see a few investigators, pass out a few Spanish versions of the Ensign (Liahona), and remind some more members about the baptisms. We got back to the chapel an hour and a half later, thinking that we would still have plenty of time before the baptisms. We walked into the chapel and there was about two inches of water all over the floor. It was soaked. We frantically grabbed some brooms and squeegees and started to sweep the water out. The floor dried just in time. The baptismal service began and things seemed to be going all right. However, we then found the gas heater had broken so that no hot water came out. The water in the font was freezing! I got down in it and about screamed. My teeth were chattering. Lorena, the fourteen year old daughter, was the first to go down the stairs into the font. She was also shivering. As I raised my hand and began saying the baptismal prayer, a miracle took place! The water was totally transformed from cold to warm. I did not even notice the coldness after that. The water stayed that way until after everyone was baptized. A total of five members of the family were converted. It was such an awesome experience, and I could feel the Spirit very strongly.

This baptism was one of the most memorable ones of my mission. I learned what a little righteousness, faith, and work can do.

For me, going on a mission, learning Spanish, and leaving my family were all very difficult. But I had faith, and God was watching over me. Now I have developed more faith, I have grown a lot, and my Spanish has become better.

How can we increase our faith? By the same manner in which we develop and improve other abilities: by studying, practicing, and working on it. By doing it we become better. Acquiring, developing, and retaining faith is a lifelong process. We must constantly do what it takes to strengthen our faith. The Savior said, ". . . if ye have faith as a grain of mustard seed, . . . nothing shall be impossible unto you" (Matthew 17:20). A grain of mustard is very small, but it transforms itself into a huge tree. If we truly believe with all of our hearts, and focus on the action that is prompted by the Spirit, great things will come to pass with the Lord's help. We can even move mountains if it is a righteous desire and the action is approved of God.

Quotes

If thou canst believe, all things are possible to him that believeth (Mark 9:23).

Now faith is the substance of things hoped for, the evidence of things not seen (Heb. 11:1).

Faith saves and miracles are wrought by its power (Gayland Jones).

Faith is not to have a perfect knowledge of things; therefore if ye have faith ye hope for things which are not seen, which are true (Alma 32:21).

By faith all things are possible with God and with man. (Joseph F. Smith, MS, 57:609).

Faith is a gift of God; it is the fruitage of righteous living. It does not come to us by command but is the result of doing the will of our Heavenly Father. (George Albert Smith, CR, October 1913, p. 103).

Faith is a gift of God bestowed as a reward for personal righteousness. It is always given when righteousness is present, and the greater the measure of obedience to God's laws the greater will be the endowment of faith. (Bruce R. McConkie, Mormon Doctrine, Salt Lake City: Bookcraft, 1966, p. 264).

Faith is nurtured through knowledge of God. It comes from prayer and feasting upon the words of Christ through diligent study of the scriptures. (Russell M. Nelson, Ensign, May 1988, p. 34).

Faith is the first great governing principle which has power, dominion, and authority over all things. (Joseph Smith, Lectures on Faith, N. B. Lundwall, comp., Salt Lake City: N. B. Lundwall, 1:24).

Great buildings were never constructed on uncertain foundations. Great causes were never brought to success by vacillating leaders. The gospel was never expounded to the convincing of others without certainty. Faith, which is of the very essence of personal conviction, has always been, and always must be, at the root of religious practice and endeavor. (Gordon B. Hinckley, Ensign, November 1981, p. 6).

Book of Mormon

"We have not been using the Book of Mormon as we should. Our homes are not as strong unless we are using it to bring our children to Christ. Our families may be corrupted by worldly trends and teachings unless we know how to use the book to expose and combat the falsehoods in socialism, organic evolution, rationalism, humanism, and so forth. Our missionaries are not as effective unless they are 'hissing forth' with it. Social, ethical, cultural, or educational converts will not survive under the heat of the day unless their taproots go down to the fullness of the gospel which the Book of Mormon contains" (Ezra Taft Benson).

The Book of Mormon is actually a volume of sacred scripture. It contains the fullness of the everlasting gospel. The purpose of the Book of Mormon is to bear record that Jesus is the Christ and Savior of the world, to teach the doctrines of the gospel in a clear manner, and to stand as a witness that Joseph Smith was a prophet of God who restored the gospel.

The prophet Joseph Smith wrote in his journal: "I told the brethren that the Book of Mormon was the most correct of any book on earth, and the keystone of our religion, and a man would get nearer to God by abiding by its precepts, than by any other book."

We actually "believe the Book of Mormon to be the word of God" (Eighth Article of Faith). The Lord said, "He (Joseph Smith) has translated the book, even that part which I have commanded him, and as your Lord and your God liveth it is true" (D&C 17:6, parentheses added). Also, many witnesses testified that they saw the plates and that the Book of Mormon is true. However, the divinity of the Book of Mormon is really evidenced in the testimony of the Spirit to the person who wants to know the truth. Moroni promised in Moroni 10:4 that, "When ye shall receive these things, I would exhort you that ye would ask God, the Eternal Father, in the name of Christ, if these things are not true; and if ye shall ask with a sincere heart, with real intent, having faith in Christ, he will manifest the truth of it unto you, by the power of the Holy Ghost."

Knowing that the Book of Mormon is the word of God, we must use this great tool in the missionary work. Help your investigators put Moroni's promise to the test by praying about its validity. The Book of Mormon was actually written for our day, and there are people all over the world who are searching for the truth but do not know where to find it. The Book of Mormon is where to find the truth.

Traits of a Good Teacher

Seeks and heeds the promptings of the Spirit of the Lord (1 Cor. 2:10-12; D&C 42:14).

Lives as an example of obedience and humility (Mosiah 23:14).

Teaches the principles of the gospel in their purity (3 Ne. 27:10-11; D&C 43:15-16; 88:77).

Loves the Lord and seeks to learn and obey His word (John 14:15; 2 Tim. 2:15; Alma 17:2-3; D&C 11:21).

Knows and loves each class member (John 13:34).

Hears, reads, and ponders the messages of the living prophets (D&C 1:37-38).

Teaches from the scriptures and approved lesson materials (D&C 42:12).

Seeks the Lord's help while preparing (D&C 50:21-25).

Seeks constantly to improve learning by adding interest, spiritual insight, and relevance (1 Cor. 14:8-9).

Gives each class member an opportunity to participate (D&C 88:122).

Helps class members apply gospel teachings in their individual lives (1 Ne. 19:23-24).

Bears witness of the truth (D&C 18:34-36).
(Instructions for Priesthood and Auxiliary Leaders on Teacher Development).

Boldness

The apostle Paul said, "For I am not ashamed of the gospel of Christ: for it is the power of God unto salvation to every one that believeth; to the Jew first, and also to the Greek" (Romans 1:16).

We know that the only way for every member of the human race to return again to our Father in Heaven is through Jesus Christ. He is the way, the truth, and the light. As missionaries, we are called to preach the gospel unto the people. We cannot be timid, shy, or afraid. We have nothing to be ashamed of. In fact, we have everything to gain and nothing to lose.

We need to be as the apostles Peter and John in the fourth chapter of Acts. They spoke boldly unto the people, the priests, the captain of the temple, and the Sadducees. A huge gathering of people was assembled there, and the number of men was about five thousand. Now this was no small group of just lower-class people. This group consisted of men in high and powerful positions. Also, five thousand is an immense number of people to be talking to. It is much larger, and probably more scary to talk to, than the largest Sacrament Meeting. In fact, it is about twelve or thirteen times as large.

In return for the many truthful things that these apostles uttered that day, they were arrested and held until the next day. However, Peter and John were filled with the Holy Ghost and preached about Christ. They declared that it was Jesus Christ of Nazareth whom the Jews crucified, and He is the only way for any man to be saved. When the people saw the boldness of

Peter and John, they marvelled. The apostles said, "For we cannot but speak the things which we have seen and heard" (Acts 4:20). They were again threatened, but were let go because they had done nothing wrong. Peter and John left and told their own people, who prayed to God together that He would grant unto Peter and John the boldness that they might speak His word. When they had prayed, the place was shaken where they were assembled together. Peter and John were filled with the Holy Ghost, and they spoke the word of God with boldness. The multitude of those that believed were of one heart and one soul. The apostles continued to preach with boldness. They performed many miracles and converted and baptized many souls. Every day, in every house, and everywhere they went, they did not cease to teach and preach about Jesus Christ.

We can see that a little boldness goes a long way. Just open your mouth. You will not feel bad for sharing your feelings and knowledge. Nor will you regret anything. The people who pay attention and hear you will feel the power of the Spirit and will probably join the church. You can touch many lives and prosper much by being bold.

Work With All Your Might

"One of the greatest secrets of missionary work is work. If a missionary works, he will get the Spirit, he will teach by the Spirit; and if he teaches by the Spirit, he will touch the hearts of the people; and he will be happy. There will be no homesickness, no worrying about families, for all time and talents and interests are centered on the work of the ministry. That's the secret—work, work, work. There is no satisfactory substitute, especially in missionary work" (President Ezra Taft Benson).

"Brethren, we don't ask HOW, WHEN, nor WHY; our question is WHY NOT? May the Lord, whose work this is, bless us, inspire us, direct us, and permit us to bring to pass His work; let's lengthen our stride and accelerate our responsibility of bringing to pass His purposes. Again, I testify to you that He will open the doors and that we can trust in His promises. I know that He will remove all opposition, He will soften the hearts, and He will prepare the path always that we have faith and persevere. Let's add to our vocabulary the expression: why not? and finally, let's lengthen the stride" (President Spencer W. Kimball).

I was first called to be Zone Leader a little over halfway through my mission. I felt a great mantle of responsibility on my shoulders. I yearned to do what I could to have a successful zone. I felt that first the missionaries needed to look inward and overcome personal problems or challenges, and then they could look outward to help investigators to progress towards baptism. I searched many books and reference materials, and pondered much about what I could do to lead the missionary work in my zone. I came up with an incredibly effective plan. This plan is entitled "The Plan of Power."

The Plan of Power

First Week: BETTERMENT

> Purpose: To focus on the Atonement. Apply the principles of repentance in our lives.

> How?:
> 1) Read selected passages from the "White Bible" (Missionary Handbook).
> 2) Purge ourselves of all indignity, pride, selfishness, and gossip.

Second Week: BE EXACT

Purpose: To focus on obeying all of the mission rules and being exact. Gain the power of obedience.

How?:
1) Make a list of all the rules that you have violated and plan how you are going to live "exact."
2) Avoid watching television and listening to the radio.
3) Fast and pray to be exact.

Third Week: SPIRITUALITY

Purpose: To focus on being on the same wavelength as the Spirit and to recognize his aid. Fast for spirituality.

How?:
1) Study/Have: Desire + Motive + Attitude = Pure Heart.
2) Utilize the Spirit.
3) Talk about Baptism with everyone every day.
4) Increase your effort and sincerity in your prayers.

Fourth Week: POWER!

Purpose: To focus on the power of Faith and use it in your work.

How?:
1) Faith.
2) Testify and challenge.
3) Be a missionary with power.

Go and get 'em! You can baptize!

When I was in the office as assistant to the president, my companion, Elder Fisk, and I decided that we needed to be the examples to all of the other missionaries in the mission, so, we tried to get our work done and get out of the office as soon as possible.

We had been working very hard for about a month, but the work was quite slow. We had a tough time finding good contacts, and the few investigators that we did have seemed to not be progressing at all. To top it all off, it was the middle of summer, and we had been stomping the streets and sweating to death without much success. We had been assigned a wealthier section of town, but we just knew that we would be able to find somebody willing to listen to our wonderful message. We just had to do it, in order to be examples to others in the mission.

Suddenly, it all hit at once. One hot summer's day, we finally found two "golden" contacts. Elder Fisk and I didn't have much time because we had an appointment for a discussion in half of an hour. We decided to hurry and knock a certain block that we had chosen. However, we did not make it around the entire block. In fact, we only made it to the second door, the last one before we had to go to our discussion. That is when we knocked and found Ana and Natalia Pezzella. It is funny how the Lord wants you to prove your willingness and diligence. He waits until the last moment, the very last door, before He honors your faith and you find those people who are searching for the truth. But it sure is worth it!

The Pezzella's invited us in, and we had a great discussion! They were so interested and asked so many questions. We were able to share simple truths that put their minds at ease. A strong spirit was felt, and their enthusiasm encouraged our hope of their learning and progression. We continued with the teaching of the discussions.

We had been a little down and depressed before that from working so hard without success. However, by working diligently, as this example shows, we were able to find success as instruments in the Lord's hands. We started finding more investigators. They were very interested and progressed more rapidly. The work was moving in leaps and bounds!

While an assistant to the president, my companion and I drafted a chart of goals. We used parts from Hartman Rector, Jr.'s book *Already to Harvest*.

The Harvest Time is Now. Open Your Mouth and Do Something Big!

1. In the month of January, in our companionship, we are having: fifteen BAPTISMS.
2. We yearn for these baptisms.
3. They are all we think and talk about.
4. We take on "all comers" in baptisms.
5. We have the "vision".
6. We take maximum advantage of every moment to achieve them.
7. We put forth unheard of physical and mental exertion.
8. We teach them boldly, skillfully, and in the spirit of love.
9. We testify with power and challenge at all times.
10. We will teach fifty discussions a week (seven per day).
11. We conclude each day with the satisfaction that another person has been baptized.
12. When we think we are too tired, that is when we receive our second wind.
13. We will have a "SUPER WEEK" (fasting and working P-day).

14. Leave at 5:00 A.M. and get back at 11:00 P.M. every day.
15. Friday we work all day.
16. We blow through ALL obstacles that Satan puts in our path and baptize these people.
17. We are in a solemn covenant with the Lord to baptize 15 souls.
18. Right now, as we plan, the Powers of Heaven are being mobilized to bring about these conversions.
19. And how great shall be our joy with them in the kingdom of our Father.

Belief plus the action that goes with it becomes faith.

President Kimball's prayer:
"Oh, our beloved Father in Heaven, bring about the day when we may be able to bring in large numbers as Ammon and his brethren did. Thousands of conversions, not dozens, not tens or fives or ones, thousands of conversions. The Lord promised it. He fulfills His promises."

Teach so your investigator receives his testimony during the discussion.

Do It! (President Kimball)

(Approved and authorized by the Assistants, Elder Jones and Elder Fisk).

In the last area of my mission, about one month before I was to return home, something great and marvelous happened. I told my companion, Elder Ishee, that I wanted to have a lot of success before my mission concluded. I did not want to be like many of the other missionaries who became "trunky" the last few months of their missions. My desire was to finish strong and endure to the end, as we are taught.

I was again called to be Zone Leader, and my job was to help the other missionaries become motivated to find, teach, and baptize. Two districts were under my responsibility. One Tuesday morning, we walked three blocks from our apartment down to the beach to ride the bus to a District Meeting. This was our custom once every week. The weather was horrible! The rain was coming down so hard that we almost got blown over just during a three-block walk. Some of the signs were blown down, broken, or shattered.

We finally arrived at the chapel for our meeting. Only two members of the district showed up besides my companion and I, so we waited for a few minutes. The District Leader decided that the rest of the missionaries were not going to show up on a day like this; therefore, he began giving the lesson on inviting investigators to make commitments during the discussions. Then, I stood up and explained that what we really needed was to sacrifice and work hard. Our missions are short and this is the Lord's time. We have to take advantage of every opportunity that arises. We cannot be like the missionaries that did not come to the District Meeting. After my talk, we closed the meeting and left to fulfill our missionary duties.

As we left the chapel, we noticed that many electricity cables and some very large trees had been knocked down. In fact, hundreds of the trees were yanked out of the ground by their roots and were lying all over. It would be a very interesting and dangerous day ahead of us. We were optimistic, though, and we had appointments to keep.

At one house, we taught a second discussion, and the husband and wife were committed to baptism. He had to bucket water from his house every five minutes because of leaks in his roof. Afterwards, we continued to check on contacts and strike up conversations with the very few people who were outside. We did teach some discussions, however, and got another baptismal date from a young lady. After a few hours of being out in the storm, we were sopping wet. We did not mind, though, and doggedly pressed on. We went to a little green and white house and knocked on the door. A middle-aged lady opened the door and just stood there in amazement, looking at the water dropping from our overcoats. She must have thought that we were crazy, but hurried and invited us in. She just could not believe that two young, North American boys would be out on a day like this. Her two teenage boys came out from their rooms to meet us. We introduced ourselves and they gave us towels to dry off with. They were also astonished. They all were very curious about these strange boys in a far-off land teaching religion in a foreign tongue. One of the boys loved the United States, so we built a very good relationship with them from the start. They offered us lunch, and we taught them the first discussion. It was a great experience to meet with them and teach them that day.

After working non-stop for the entire day, we returned home to rest. We were very tired. By listening to the news on a neighbor's TV, we found out that the wind reached speeds of 120 kilometers per hour (75 mph), many people were without light and water, and three people had been killed. We had indeed sacrificed ourselves that day to the Lord. He blessed us beyond comprehension. We had made many contacts, taught many discussions, set three baptismal dates, and found an incredible family of three who all were baptized at a later date. It was interesting that part of our area was flooded. We could not get in and the people could not get out. However, we had fun the whole day, even being drenched and bogged down in the mud. I would say that we were very blessed, and had an incredible day due to our sacrifices and hard work!

Don't Quit

When things go wrong as they sometimes will, when the road you are trudging seems all up hill,
when the funds are low and the debts are high, and you want to smile but you have to sigh.
When care is pressing you down a bit, rest if you must, but don't you quit!

Life is queer with its twists and turns, as everyone of us sometimes learns, and many a failure turns about,
when he might have won had he stuck it out.
Don't give up though the pace seems slow, you may succeed with another blow.

Success is failure turned inside out, the silver tint of the clouds of doubt.
And you never can tell how close you are, it may be near when it seems so far.
So stick to the fight when you are hardest hit, it's when things seem worse that you must not quit!

Quotes

There is an election going on all the time. The Lord votes for you and Satan votes against you. You decide the winning vote (Anonymous).

If you believe you can or believe you cannot, you are right (Henry Ford).

The Ph.D. for missionary work is . . . Prayer, Humility, Diligence (Anonymous).

The only job where you start at the top is digging a hole (Anonymous).

The message of missionaries is the most important message in the world—it saves souls (Gayland Jones).

You are going out on your mission, not merely to make friends for the Church, though that is important, but to properly convert and baptize the numerous people who are anxious and ready for the gospel. Brethren, the spirit of our work must be urgency, and we must imbue our missionaries and saints with this spirit of "Now." We are not justified in waiting for the natural, slow growth which would come with natural and easy proselyting . . . . We believe that we must put our shoulder to the wheel, lengthen our stride, heighten our reach, increase our devotion so that we can do the work to which we have been assigned (Spencer W. Kimball, Quoted by Bruce R. McConkie, Mission Presidents' Seminar, June 21, 1976).

Even a clock passes the time by keeping its hands busy (Anonymous).

Our days are like identical suitcases—all the same size but some people can pack more into them than others (Anonymous).

If you are going to kill time, work it to death (Anonymous).

We have been given one mouth and two ears so that we can listen twice as well as we can talk (Gayland Jones).

Mind over mattress (Anonymous).

A smooth path might get you there faster, but a rough path will teach you more (Anonymous).

When you are down, look up (Anonymous).

A smile is a curve that sets a lot of things straight (Anonymous).

There are no traffic jams on the extra mile (Anonymous).

Until one is committed, there is hesitancy, a chance to draw back. But, the moment one definitely commits oneself, then God moves too, and a whole stream of events erupts—all manner of unforeseen incidents, meetings, persons, material assistance—begin to flow toward him (David O. McKay).

The missionaries who spend the least money and accept the simple hospitality of the people, accomplish the most work, develop the greatest faith and obtain the greatest results (Sylvester Q. Cannon, CR, October 1938, p. 96).

If you will double the number of investigators at church, you will double the number of baptisms (Anonymous).

The principles of the gospel...should be presented to men in humility, in the simplest forms of speech, without presumption or arrogance and in the spirit of the mission of Christ . . . . By earnestness and simplicity missionaries will establish themselves in the truth, [and their] testimonies will convince others . . . . They will touch the hearts of the people and will have the pleasure of seeing them come to an understanding of their message. The spirit of the gospel will shine forth from their souls and others will partake of their light and rejoice therein. (Joseph F. Smith, CR, April 1899, p. 40).

The work of a missionary is everlasting in its consequences. Acceptance of the gospel at the hands of a true and dedicated teacher affects not only the recipient, but also generations who come after the recipient. (Gordon B. Hinckley, Ensign, May 1983, p. 85).

Remember, you go into the mission field to baptize, not just to warn or make friends. Your goal is to bring people to Christ and proclaim the truth. Nothing more, nothing less (Ed J. Pinegar).

Leadership Through Example

These are some duties that are expected of you. To be a successful leader, there are FIVE KEYS:

1. Be the top baptizer.
2. Be the best teacher.
3. Be the most humble.
4. Love the people with all your heart.
5. Work harder than anyone else.

As a leader, the missionaries will always have a great respect for you. A leader should always radiate love and a special excitement for the missionary work. He understands the importance of his sacred calling. Never let the other missionaries see you down or depressed; always radiate a positive attitude. Know of the example that you are demonstrating and always find yourself doing the appropriate thing. You should always ask yourself:

1. Am I being a good example?
2. Am I worthy to receive the direction of the Lord?
3. Am I doing all that I can to motivate others?
4. Am I doing all that I can to support the growth of my companion, the area, and myself?
5. Do I really love all the missionaries in my zone?
6. Am I planning effectively?
7. Am I charitable?

Leadership is not something you do *to* people, but rather something you do *with* people. Leaders need to do what those they supervise cannot do for themselves at the present moment.

Christ

Christ has done His part, are you doing yours?

Christ never said it would be easy, He only said it would be worth it.

The first quote I am sure you have heard before. While in the MTC, I saw this every single day as I was coming to or going from my dormitory. There is a square frame on the bottom floor of every building on the campus. On the left side of the frame is a picture of Christ. On the right side of the frame is a mirror. As you stand there, you see your refection right by Christ's picture. This picture would seem to jump out at me all the time. I knew that Christ had done His part, and I was striving to do mine. This idea was a great reminder that the Lord had died for me and I should be willing to do everything that I could, for at least two years, to further His work.

D&C 122:7-8 says, ". . . know thou, my son, that all these things shall give thee experience, and shall be for thy good. The Son of Man hath descended below them all. Art thou greater than he?" I really feel humble knowing that Christ paid the price for me, and that I will be indebted to Him forever. I should at least do my part noting that it won't be easy, but it will be worth it, as the second quote says.

One Solitary Life

He was born in an obscure village, the child of a peasant

woman. He grew up in still another village, where He worked in a carpenter shop until He was thirty. Then for three years He was an itinerant preacher. He never wrote a book. He never held an office. He never had a family or owned a house. He didn't go to college. He never visited a big city. He never traveled more than two hundred miles from the place where He was born.

He did none of the things one usually associates with greatness. He had no credentials but himself. He was only thirty-three when the tide of public opinion turned against Him. His friends ran away. He was turned over to His enemies and went through the mockery of a trial. He was nailed to a cross between two thieves. While He was dying, His executioners gambled for His clothing; the only property He had on Earth. When He was dead, He was laid in a borrowed grave through the pity of a friend.

Nineteen centuries have come and gone, and today He is the central figure of the human race and the leader of mankind's progress. All the armies that ever marched, all the navies that ever sailed, all the parliaments that ever sat, all the kings that ever reigned, put together, have not affected the life of man on this Earth as much as that One Solitary Life (Anonymous).

As missionaries, we are representatives of the Lord, Jesus Christ. Every day we put on our black name tags that carry his name. We always hand out pamphlets of the picture of Christ. As in 2 Nephi 25:26, "We talk of Christ, we rejoice in Christ, we preach of Christ, we prophesy of Christ, and we write according to our prophecies, that our children may know to what source they may look for a remission of their sins." In Alma 34:8-9 Amulek testifies that Christ will come and atone for the sins of all mankind. Then, He came to confirm the fulfillment of that prophecy, for we read in 3 Nephi 11 of the appearance of Christ in the Americas after his resurrection. He showed the prints of the nails in His hands and feet to the people. By being baptized and building our foundation on His rock, we can follow His perfect example. And finally, we ask the investigators to follow His example and be baptized. By way of Christ's sacrifice and atonement, we can all be saved from sin, repent, and find peace in this life.

I would like to review a little of what Christ went through for us: First, Christ knew that he would have to endure the atonement, so he went to the Garden of Gethsemane to pray and fulfill his Father's will. Luke relates the event in chapter 22:41-44. No other mortal being could have experienced this event and survived. This exposed skin would send the person into excruciating pain, even if a handkerchief were placed on it.

Next, he was accused of heresy and had His trial before Pilate. Pilate, finding him innocent, left it in the hands of the people as they cried, "Crucify him, crucify him." So they took Him to be wounded and beaten. They punished Him by scourging—two soldiers whipped His bare skin. The whips had chipped bones, glass, and balls on them. Christ was whipped as much as the Roman law allowed: thirty-nine times. They rammed a crown of thorns into His head. Then, tired and beaten, they made Him carry His own cross to Calvary. He fainted in the trek. After this came the crucifixion. The soldiers pounded spikes into His hands, wrists, and feet. What excruciating pain! Then they dropped the pole into the ground. The force must have ripped His flesh. Everything that happened on the cross compounded the experience at Gethsemane.

The last statements that He made while the soldiers were wagering bets on his clothes were: 1) "Woman, behold thy son" (John 19:26-27), 2) "I thirst" (:28), 3) "Father, forgive them; for they know not what they do" (Luke 23:34), 4) "Verily I say unto thee, today shalt thou be with me in paradise" (:43), 5) "My God, my God, why hast thou forsaken me?" (Mark 15:34), 6) "It is finished" (John 19:30), and 7) "Father, into thy hands I commend my spirit" (Luke 23:46).

I wrote the following poem while pondering about our Savior and Redeemer, Jesus Christ. Without Him we are literally nothing. He is THE most important figure in the history of the world. I have much gratitude in my heart for Him, and strive to become like Him more each day.

Never a Better Friend

The night is dark and there almost is no light,
but in my house is a fire lit and a picture there of Christ.
Now I'm going on a mission soon and two years will be my stay,
and I know I cannot make it without His help day by day.

My mind starts to drift away and think about this man, who never committed even one bad deed but yet died by soldier hands.
He did his part even more than I can comprehend, He gave of Himself voluntarily so my life would not have an end.

He sweat great drops of blood as though it wouldn't stop, and the soldiers took Him and beat Him, with whips of glassened tops.
There was never a better friend who was always by my side, who carried me when I needed it if I couldn't make the ride.

You see, this friendship is too strong to break and there will never be an end, the one who died to give me life, there is never a better friend. Then He carried a cross to a mountain crest until His body fell, and after a crown of thorns on His head, they pierced His hands with nails.

In humility He said, "Father, forgive them for they know not what they do." I know I'm all alone in this, but after, I'll be back again with you.
The Spirit, love, and testimonies are the seeds that help me grow, into a man, a missionary, and whom Jesus Christ I know . . .

will guide me to a foreign land with people all unknown, and help me spread His message—with His help I'm not alone.
The life I've found, the light I've seen, leads me on my way, it brings me closer to my Lord and Savior more and more each day.
When my time comes, there will be a day, that signifies the end, but only of my first two years that Christ was my best friend.

Love

In my third area, I found myself in the city of Tandil. My companion, Elder Miller, was a young, yet exceptional, missionary. We taught each other many things, and we were very much the same in many aspects.

As we were out knocking doors one day, we came to a one-room house. It was a very humble home. One could tell that the family didn't have a lot of money. In fact, the house was made of cinderblock and had a tin roof. There was no paint or decorations on or around the house. In place of the door, there was only a hanging sheet. You can imagine the environment there.

We walked to the entrance of a fence that lined the dirt street. My companion clapped his hands, for that was the Argentine way of knocking at gates. We waited for a few moments, and then a teen-age boy came out. We told him who we were and that we wanted to talk to the entire family. He said that he was the only one home. We tried to extract a little information from him, but to no avail, so we looked at each other and then left. As my companion and I continued walking, we conversed about our impressions to return to that house.

Day after day went by, and we visited that home almost every day without fail. Different members of the family kept coming to the door with trivial excuses. It seemed like they did not want any part of what we had to say. All they did was avoid us. However, my companion and I felt differently about the situation. We knew that we needed to continue returning to see them. We did not know what would result from our actions, but we had to keep bothering them. Sometimes you just have to do that.

Finally, the day came that the mother invited us in to find out who we were. Maybe the Lord had softened her heart, or maybe she was just so sick and tired of us that she wanted to get it over with. Whatever the case may be, she did invite us in and we were very happy about that. Our discussion was a little different than the formal first discussion that a missionary is accustomed to giving. The mother was trying to raise her two boys alone. Neither she nor they had jobs, and one of the boys had some mental disabilities. We discussed their many problems and tried to share our message. We knew that the gospel could help them, but they were more concerned about survival first. How could they accept baptism when they may not have food on the table that night? They could not. Certain priorities come first. We finished our discussion and arranged for a time to return.

The weather changed quite drastically, and it started to rain very hard. We walked half a block and found shelter under a grocery store's canopy. Elder Miller and I tried to wait out the storm. As we turned to look at each other, we both had the same idea. We entered the store and began searching the aisles. This family and their challenges were very much on our minds. We did not have a lot of money, but we wanted to buy them some food. The milk, bread, noodles, and beans all seemed to jump out at us. We made our purchases and went back to the Morales' house, set the food just inside the door and ran off so that they would not know who did it.

The next day we returned to visit with them and continue with the discussions. We nonchalantly went up to their door. The mom, Blanca, opened the curtain. The first thing that she asked was, "Did you boys give us that food last night?" We both just stared at her and smiled. She had so much gratitude that she could not thank us enough. That act of love and service was what broke the ice. Many people respond differently to different things, and at different times in their lives. The Morales family needed that food at that time, and that act of compassion was what built our relationship of trust.

We proceeded to teach them the discussions and make them feel comforted. We gave assistance wherever we could. In fact, the mother and younger son both acquired jobs. They found a better home that they were going to rent, and we helped them move all of their belongings to the new place. They did not have a truck and trailer, let alone a car, so we used our arms, wagons, and wheelbarrows. That experience was so great that I will never forget it. Indeed, it was a lot of fun.

By caring and loving this wonderful family, they saw what good people we were. They had considerable respect and trust for us. Our love radiated until it sparked their interest, and they persevered until they entered into the waters of baptism. The mother bore her testimony even before she became a member. She testified to all her friends, and even came to teach discussions with us. I do know that loving the people is an essential skill to learn if you want success.

Quotes

If you cannot be with the ones you love, love the ones you are with (Anonymous).

"Love is the essence of the gospel and the guiding light for a Christlike life. It not only teaches us to look upward but also to look around us" (Hans B. Ringger, Ensign, May 1990, p. 26).

Empathy is like contact lenses. By looking through another set of eyes, you can understand the whole picture (Gayland Jones).

Companions

Geese "V" Formation Helps Birds in Flight

Next fall, when you see geese heading South for the winter flying along in a "V" formation, you might be interested in knowing what science has discovered about why they fly that way. It has been learned that as each bird flaps its wings, it creates an uplift for the bird immediately following. By flying in a "V" formation, the whole flock adds at least seventy-one percent greater flying range than if each bird flew on its own (people who share a common direction and sense of community can get where they are going quicker and easier, because they are traveling on the "thrust" of one another).

Whenever a goose falls out of formation, it suddenly feels the drag and resistance of trying to go it alone, and quickly gets into formation to take advantage of the lifting power of the bird immediately in front (if we have as much sense as a goose, we will stay in formation with those who are headed in the same way *we* are going). When the lead goose gets tired, he rotates back in the wing and another goose flies point (it pays to take turns doing hard jobs). The geese honk from behind to encourage those up front to keep up their speed (what do we say when *we* honk from behind?).

Finally (now get this), when a goose gets sick, or is wounded by gunshot and falls out, two geese fall out of formation and follow him down to help and protect him. They stay with him until he is either able to fly or until he is dead, and they then launch out on their own or with another formation to catch up with the group (if we have the sense of a goose, we will stand by each other like that).

There are times when you and your companion will not see things in the same way. You will disagree on occasion because of the differences that you have. You have to remember that you are different people with different personalities. Even though you are both members of the church serving missions, you were both brought up in different circumstances. You will have about a dozen different companions, and you will need to learn how to get along with all of them. Just remember this geese story. Communication and support are two vital keys to a successful companionship. Work things out together and protect each other.

Always have a good attitude and stand by each other! (Anonymous).

Miracles

"When the Lord said, 'Lengthen your stride, quicken your pace, heighten your reach, widen your vision, and stretch your capacity,' he was in reality saying 'expect a miracle,' for these are the stuff from which miracles are made" (Hartman Rector, Jr., Ensign, May 1979, p. 31).

Miracles are those occurrences wrought by the power of God which are wholly beyond the power of man to perform. They are actually gifts of the Spirit. Miracles are also the fruits of faith and righteousness. They are not manifest until after the foundation of faith has been securely built. "And neither at any time hath any wrought miracles until after their faith; wherefore they first believed in the Son of God" (Ether 12:18). "Thus God has provided a means that man, through faith, might work mighty miracles; therefore he becometh a great benefit to his fellow beings" (Mosiah 8:18). So, by our being obedient to the things of God, and having tremendous faith, we can literally work some great miracles. Here is an account of a man's exceedingly great faith, as well as the faith of missionaries.

While I was in the office serving as assistant, my companion and I had occasion to converse with some other elders from a different area. They said that they had recently met a guy who was a friend of a Church member they knew. His name was Cesar, and he was in the hospital. They had gone with the member friend to give him a blessing before he had an operation. They explained to us that he lived in our area, and that we could teach him the discussions when he got out of the hospital. We decided to do some splits with the other elders so that we could gradually work with him as he got better. That way it wouldn't be as much of a shock to him when my companion and I began going to his house to teach him.

After working off and on with him for a while, we decided to sit down and have an in-depth interview about his traumatic experience. We also wanted to find out where he stood with the discussions and how he felt about the Church, so we went to his house one afternoon. He was excited to see us and invited us in. We asked him about his experience in the hospital, and he told us an overwhelming story. He said that when he was younger he lived a pretty horrible life. He stayed out late, drank a lot of beer and wine, and smoked about five or six packs of cigarettes a day. He was popular with the other kids and had quite a few girlfriends. He slept around, and even had a child. However, he never married the baby's mother nor stayed with her. He sang Rock and Roll in a band, and was the national champion in the butterfly swim. We found that quite interesting because he was in such terrible shape. He was a very large man. At the time, he felt like he was happy just being like the rest of his friends. Nevertheless, he found out that his life was just the opposite. As he led this hard life, time began to wear him down and he finally found himself getting sick. His condition gradually worsened until one day he had some massive heart attacks. He found himself lying on his back in a hospital.

Cesar related his account of the events that happened to him that terrible day. He said that he must have blacked out because he could not remember how he arrived at the hospital or why he was there. Nonetheless, he had a dream experience that he could remember. He explained that his surroundings got very dark and that he was in great despair. Suddenly, a bright light appeared, and he saw himself on the outer edge of the light. He began to walk towards this light. It was as if he talked to Heavenly Father or a heavenly messenger because he knew that he had to change his life around. They must have conversed about the gospel for a little while, and then Cesar came to. He remembered that the doctors were shocking him so that he would come back to life. He had a near-death experience—basically, he had died and then come back to receive the gospel.

Cesar knew that he must change and become a righteous person. He just knew that he had to take the discussions. Those feelings were why he had the surety that we were missionaries sent from God. He believed everything that we were teaching him. In fact, he knew that ours was the true church. We helped him feel the Spirit, and he committed to being baptized. Cesar was preparing every day, and he even sent us a dedication over his radio program. That action was very special to me, because his program was the most popular of ten such programs in the city of five hundred thousand people.

The day finally came for Cesar Saud to be baptized and become a member of The Church of Jesus Christ of Latter-day Saints. He was going to enter the door that leads to exaltation. We wrote up programs and invited many people. The service was great, and it was about the most well-attended baptism that I had ever seen while on my mission. Cesar was a little nervous and he had to be immersed twice, but it was so special. He glowed from head to toe.

After his baptism, Cesar was very grateful and treated us like his own sons. He invited us to speak on his radio program, had us over for dinner and birthdays, and gave us gifts. However, the most amazing part about Cesar was that he was growing in the gospel. His testimony was increasing and becoming stronger. He began to teach the gospel to his friends. We had more baptisms because of it. He received the priesthood, baptized and confirmed other people, and became the second counselor in the Sunday School presidency. Cesar Saud was an extraordinary man!

"Miracles are one of the great evidences of the divinity of the Lord's work. Where there are true miracles, there is the true church; where these miracles are not, there the true church is not" (Bruce R. McConkie, Mormon Doctrine, p. 507). God is the same yesterday, today, and forever. If He performed miracles in ancient times, He will certainly perform them today. He does not change or vary, so the day of miracles has not ceased.

As a missionary, I would develop and increase my faith; then I would go out expecting miracles based on that faith, through obedience and hard work.

Return With Honor

The best way to return home from a mission is with the knowledge deep down in your heart that you have given your all for two years. If you do not regret anything, then you know that you will feel pleased about your mission in the service of the Lord.

The Marks of a Man

The taxi pulled up to the front doors of the airport just as the final boarding call for my flight was made. I was flying from Miami to Salt Lake City and was delayed by a long company meeting. I ran and jumped on board, then stopped for a minute to catch my breath.

Near the front of the plane sat an excited young man, probably nineteen, sitting with his parents. His hair was short and his clothes were new and sharp. His suit was fitted perfectly and his black shoes still retained that store-bought shine. His body was in good shape, his hands clean. In his eyes I could see a nervous look, and his movements were that of an actor on opening night.

He was obviously flying to Utah to become a missionary for the Mormon church. I smiled as I walked by and took pride in belonging to this same church where these young men voluntarily serve the Savior for two years. With this special feeling I made my way back to where my seat was located.

As I sat down, I looked to the right and to my surprise

saw another missionary sleeping in the window seat. His hair was also short, but that was the only similarity between the two. This one was obviously returning home, and I could tell at a glance what type of missionary he had been.

The fact that he was already asleep told me a lot. His entire body seemed to let out a big sigh. It looked as if this was the first time in two years he had ever slept, and I wouldn't be surprised if it was.

As I looked at his face, I could see the heavy bags under his eyes, the chapped lips, and the leathery sunburned face caused by the fierce Florida sun.

His suit was tattered and worn. A few of the seams were coming apart, and I noticed that there were a couple of rips that had been hand-sewn with a very sloppy stitch.

I saw the name tag; crooked, scratched and bearing the name of the church he represented, the engraving of which was almost all worn away. I saw the knees of his pants, worn and white, the result of many hours of humble prayer.

A tear came to my eye as I saw the things that really told me what kind of missionary he had been. I saw the marks that made this boy a man.

His feet, the two that had carried him from house to house, now lay there swollen and tired. They were covered by a pair of worn-out shoes. Many large scrapes and gouges had been filled in by countless numbers of polishings.

His books, laying across his side, were his scriptures—the word of God. Once new, these books which testify of Jesus Christ and His mission, were now torn, bent, and ragged from use.

His hands—those big, strong hands which had been used to bless and teach, were now scarred and the knuckles cut from knocking.

Those were indeed the marks of that man. As I looked at

him I saw the marks of another man, the Savior, as He was hanging on the cross for the sins of the world.

His feet—that had once carried Him throughout the land during His ministry, were now nailed to the cross. His side—pierced with a spear, sealing His gospel and His testimony with His life. His hands—that had been used to ordain His disciples, bless the sick, and raise the dead were also scarred with the nails pounded into the cross.

Those were indeed the marks of that great man.

As my mind returned to thoughts of the missionary, my whole body seemed to swell with pride and joy, because I knew by looking at him, that he had served his master well.

My joy was so great. I felt like running to the front of the plane, grabbing that new young missionary, and bringing him back to see what he can become; what he could do.

But would he see those things as I did? Would anyone see the things I saw? Or would he just see the outward appearance of that mighty elder, tired and worn-out.

As we landed, I reached over and tapped him to wake him up. As he awoke, it seemed like new life was entering his body. His whole frame just seemed to fill and he sat up, tall and proud. As he turned his face towards mine, I saw a light about his face that I had never seen before. I looked into his eyes. I will never forget those eyes—they were the eyes of a prophet, a leader, a follower, and a servant. They were the eyes of the Savior. No words were spoken. No words were needed.

As we unloaded, I stepped aside to let him go first. I watched as he walked, slow, but steady; tired, yet strong. I followed him and found myself walking the way he did.

When I came through the doors, I saw this young man in the arms of his parents, and I couldn't hold my emotions any longer. With tears streaming down my face, I watched those loving parents greet their son who had been away for a short time, and I wondered if our parents in Heaven would greet us the same way. Will they wrap their arms around us and welcome us home from our journey? I believe they will. I just hope that I can be worthy enough to receive such praise as I'm sure this missionary will.

I said a silent prayer, thanking the Lord for all missionaries like this young man. I don't think I will ever forget the joy and happiness he brought to me that day (Anonymous).

When a missionary gets off the plane after a two-year mission, there is much joy and happiness. Some of his missionary friends are there to say their last good-byes as fellow missionaries, and his friends and loved ones are all around to welcome him home. His family is especially glad to see him. His mom will come up and throw her arms around him and rejoice in his homecoming. His brothers and sisters will be there to congratulate him, and his dad will come up and embrace him and say, "Well done, son."

This scene is an analogy showing how it is going to be when our journey here in life is finished. We will return home to our Heavenly Parents. They will greet us and embrace us. Our Heavenly Mother will be pleased, and our Father in Heaven will say, "Well done, my son."

I hope that at that final day you will be able to say with all sincerity, just like Paul, "I have fought a good fight, I have finished my course, I have kept the faith: Henceforth there is laid up for me a crown of righteousness, which the Lord, the righteous judge, shall give me at that day: and not to me only, but unto all them also that love his appearing" (2 Timothy 4: 7-8).

About the Author

Gayland R Jones graduated from Southern Utah University with a Masters of Accountancy degree. He also completed his Bachelor of Arts Composite Major in Accounting and Business Administration from that same institution, as well as earning a Spanish Minor.

Mr. Jones is presently employed as a Senior Auditor with the Utah State Auditor's Office in Salt Lake City, Utah. Mr. Jones enjoys sports, hunting, fishing, and the outdoors. Mr. Jones served an LDS mission in Bahia Blanca, Argentina. He is married to Kammie Bradshaw Jones. They have a daughter named Arianna, and they reside in Taylorsville, Utah.

CEDAR FORT, INCORPORATED
Order Form

Name: _____

Address: _____

City: _____ State: _____ Zip: _____

Phone: ( ) _____ Daytime phone: ( ) _____

Fight the Good Fight

Quantity: _____ @ $9.95 each: _____

plus $3.49 shipping & handling for the first book: _____

(add 99¢ shipping for each additional book)

Utah residents add 6.25% for state sales tax: _____

TOTAL: _____

Bulk purchasing, shipping and handling quotes available upon request.

Please make check or money order payable to:
Cedar Fort, Incorporated.

Mail this form and payment to:
Cedar Fort, Inc.
925 North Main St.
Springville, UT 84663

You can also order on our website **www.cedarfort.com**
or e-mail us at sales@cedarfort.com or call 1-800-SKYBOOK